PLANT KINGDOMS

THE PHOTOGRAPHS OF CHARLES JONES

PLANT KINGDOMS
THE PHOTOGRAPHS OF CHARLES JONES

SEAN SEXTON - ROBERT FLYNN JOHNSON

PREFACE BY ALICE WATERS

SMITHMARK

Half-title Onion Ailsa Craig, 6 x 4¹/₄ in. (152 x 108 mm)

Title page Carrot Long Red, 10 x 8 in. (254 x 203 mm)

p. 6 Mangold Yellow Globe, 6 x 4¹/₄ in. (152 x 108 mm)

p. 9 Bean Long Pod, 10 x 8 in. (254 x 203 mm)

Sean Sexton gives special thanks to the following for their help in the preparation of this book:
Philippe Garner, John Benjafield, Steffen Wolff, Andy Cowan of Hamiltons, Vanessa Kramer
and Susannah Harrison of Corbis, William A. Ewing, John McGuire, Dr. Murray MacKinnon,
Ian Jack, Nick Burnett, David Robinson, Jennifer Vine. Warmest thanks in addition to Clarissa
Bruce for her photography.

Published by arrangement with Thames and Hudson Ltd, London

This edition published in 1998 by SMITHMARK Publishers,
a division of U.S. Media Holdings, Inc.,
115 West 18ᵗʰ Street, New York, NY 10011.

SMITHMARK books are available for bulk purchase
for sales promotion and premium use.
For details write or call the manager of special sales,
SMITHMARK Publishers, 115 West 18ᵗʰ Street, New York, NY 10011.

ISBN 0-7651-0836-4

Printed in Singapore

10 9 8 7 6 5 4 3 2 1

Library of Congress Cataloging-In-Publication Data

Jones, Charles, 1866–1959.
        Plant kingdoms : the photographs of Charles Jones / Sean Sexton,
    Robert Flynn Johnson ; preface by Alice Waters.
            p.   cm.
        Includes bibliographical references (p.   ).
        ISBN 0-7651-0836-4
        1. Photography of plants.   2. Jones, Charles, 1866–1959.
    3. Vegetables—Pictorial works.   4. Flowers—Pictorial works.
    5. Fruit—Pictorial works.   I. Sexton, Sean.   II. Johnson, Robert
    Flynn.   III. Title.
    TR724.J65   1998
    779'.34'092—dc21   98–7286

CONTENTS

PREFACE by Alice Waters

A bunch of radishes. A bunch of grapes. A single turnip. A stack of heads of cauliflower. Several tomatoes, still on the vine. When I first saw these images by Charles Jones, they took my breath away. His portraits of nature are the surviving artifacts of a sensibility so reverent of, and so exquisitely attuned to, the overwhelming beauty of the fruits of the earth, that any cook with a passion for pure and fresh ingredients must be grateful that these photographs have been rescued from obscurity.

Of course the photographer would have had to be a gardener, or a cook—and a good one, with a keen, unjaded eye. Who else would have composed still lifes so alive that they are hardly still at all? Any cook or kitchen gardener looking closely at them will quickly deduce that many of these subjects were photographed while yet unharvested, still growing in the ground, and the rest probably minutes afterward. The sense of aliveness the images convey is even more striking than the perfections of form and natural beauty they record. On a vine with unwilted flowers and resinous leaves, tomatoes hang like giant black pearls aglow from within. A big globular turnip rests on a flat surface, looking wide awake. Its greens have been cut off, but it is palpably smooth and firm, and it has not been scrubbed or waxed. A little dirt still clings to it. Clearly, it has been dug up, topped, and brushed clean in the very recent past.

Each of Jones' fruits, flowers, and vegetables has been posed, ravishingly, to capture the particularity and individuality of its variety. The simplicity and truthfulness of the compositions is intensified by the use of the sharpest focus and the tight close-up, with the subjects usually isolated against neutral backgrounds. Extraneous detail has been stripped away. There is no excess cabbage, and no excess of anything else. Jones concentrates our attention on the detail and singularity of just one specimen, or a representative few. Nevertheless, when he records the fava beans within a single split-open pod, he implies the basketfuls waiting to be gathered, shelled, peeled, and eaten.

Things to eat that look this vibrant are irresistible to a cook. Jones' photographs illustrate perfectly how the food most people are pleased to call "fresh"—food harvested weeks ago, transported hundreds (or thousands) of miles, refrigerated for weeks at the market and weeks more at home—cannot be compared to the real thing—food grown nearby, picked ripe today, and ready to be cooked and eaten right now.

Right now, so late in the century, when so many people are being displaced and made hungry—even while others are being urbanized and overfed on unwholesome and processed food—the art of Charles Jones reminds us that horticulture is sacred. There is no other word for it. May those of us who feast on these photographs be inspired to try and make such a bounty of good things, and such reverence for their beauty, an unalienable part of everyone's life.

1 *Charles Jones, c.* 1904, albumen print, 6 x 4¹/₄ in. (152 x 108 mm)

INTRODUCTION

by Robert Flynn Johnson

"How difficult it is to be simple."

Vincent van Gogh in a letter to Paul Gauguin, 1890 [1]

Charles Harry Jones (1) was born in England in 1866 at Wolverhampton. The son of a master butcher, Jones trained as a gardener, although where and with whom he received his early education and inspiration is not known. On February 22, 1894, at age 27, he married. During the 1890s he took a number of gardener positions in private estates, most notably Ote Hall, in the parish of Wivelsfield near Burgess Hill, Sussex.

While at Ote Hall, Charles Jones distinguished himself sufficiently to receive mention in the September 20, 1905 issue of *The Gardeners' Chronicle*:

"The present gardener, Charles Jones, has had a large share in the modelling of the gardens as they now appear for on all sides can be seen evidences of his work in the making of flowerbeds and borders and in the planting of fruit trees, etc. A beautiful herbaceous border is one of his most recent additions to the gardening features around the Hall. This border extends several hundred feet in an almost semi-circular manner and encloses the spacious lawn. Being of considerable width, it accommodates a rich and varied collection of hardy herbaceous plants so that some of them are in flower at all seasons of the year. . . . Pleasing as are these decorative portions of the gardens, the fruit and vegetable quarters are equally so and this especially applies to the fruit gardens. Mr. Jones is quite an enthusiastic fruit grower and his delight in his well-trained fruit trees was readily apparent. The majority of the fruit trees in the gardens are of his own raising, and it must be recorded that nowhere would one expect to find better examples whether bush or pyramid, espalier or cordon-trained trees. . . . The lack of extensive glass houses is no deterrent to Mr. Jones in producing supplies of choice flowers and fruits. . . . By the help of wind screens, he has converted warm nooks into suitable places for the growing of tender subjects and with the aid of a few unheated frames produces a goodly supply. Tomatoes growing in one of these sheltered corners were quite equal to those usually seen in glass structures, and inverted sea-kale covers were doing duty for pots. Thus is the resourcefulness of the ingenious gardener, who has not an unlimited supply of the best appurtenances seen." [2]

Sometime between 1904 and 1910 Jones, his wife and children left Ote Hall and resettled in Lincolnshire. His activities from that time until his death half a century later are something of a mystery. Surviving members of his family, including his grandaughter Shirley Sadler, remember Jones as an intensely private person and quite uncommunicative. Aspects of his life exist in family memories. "He supposedly made a series of photographs of Grimsthorpe Castle in Bourne. He was commissioned by one of the ministries during World War II to grow certain plants." These recollections are tantalizing, yet unverified.

By the 1950s, Jones and his wife were still living in Lincolnshire with no electricity or running water. He was a Victorian outcast who could not reconcile himself to the realities of living in a modern age. His children were shocked to find that for many years he did not claim his rightful old age pension. Always a proud man, he considered it charity. He died at age 92 on November 15, 1959. These would be the salient events of a seemingly solid, unassuming, yet useful life except for a discovery made twenty-two years later.

In 1981, at the Bermondsey antique market in London, the author and photographic collector Sean Sexton chanced upon a trunk for sale. It contained hundreds of photographs which all appeared to be of the same subject—vegetables. Though they had been passed over and scorned by dealers and collectors earlier in the day, Sexton instantly saw an originality and quality in the works, acquiring the whole collection for a nominal sum.

Whoever took the photographs was as fastidious in his notations as he was in the execution and printing of the photographs, which were gold-toned gelatin silver prints made from glass-plate negatives. Two-thirds of the images were vegetables, with the remaining third evenly divided between fruits and flowers.

Virtually all the photographs were meticulously annotated in graphite with the exact name of the plant followed by the initials "C.J." (2 and 3). A few of the photographs, however, were inscribed with the full name of the photographer . . . Charles Jones.

Unfortunately, knowing the few facts relating to Jones' life and work does not answer what may be the most fundamental questions regarding his art: how it came to pass that an obscure gardener could produce photographs of such originality and vision; how to account for the consistency of his aesthetic approach; the source (if any) of his training; where he found the time to create such a large body of work; and finally, why his achievement not only escaped contemporary notice but also remained neglected to the point that it was saved from extinction only at the very last moment. These are intriguing questions, some of which may never be answered. A particularly difficult problem will be to provide answers regarding the forging of

2   Charles Jones
British, 1866–1959
Dwarf Bean Waxpod
c. 1900
gold-toned gelatin
silver print
6 x 4¹/₄ in. (152 x 108 mm)

13

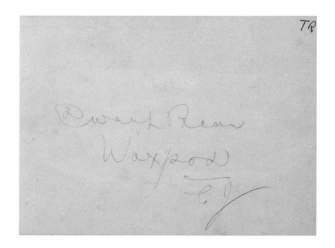

3   Charles Jones
British, 1866–1959
verso of *Dwarf Bean
Waxpod, c.* 1900
gold-toned gelatin
silver print
6 x 4¹/₄ in. (152 x 108 mm)

the artist's sensibilities. In general, of course, it would be worth taking note of the fact that gardening, like medicine, breeds keen vision in its most exemplary practitioners, and that the focus of the gardener's world is frequently on the smaller products of his or her efforts. In a certain sense, then, it is reasonable that the gardener-naturalist who attains competence in photography might become devoted to celebrating some of the most attractive aspects of the world which he or she knows so intimately.

It seems that Jones once put an ad in a journal, *Popular Gardening,* offering to take photographs of people's gardens for half-a-crown per image. Whatever came of this enterprise is not known, as very few of the surviving photographs are anything but close-up still lifes. It is also important to note that, except in a very few cases, Jones' photographs exist only in unique examples. Charles Jones obviously thought of himself as a serious photographer, or at least considered his work with sufficient artistic pride to initial each photograph carefully. Why then did he not exhibit the results? Charles Jones falls into a category now referred to as "outsider" artist. The "outsider" has energy and determination to create, but through fear of rejection or personal indifference to sharing his or her achievements with others, refuses to exhibit or even acknowledge to the world the existence of that art. To be sure, most outsider art has disappeared, for its practitioners have been successful at sealing its existence and thereby its fate. One recollection of Charles Jones' grandchildren is poignant. At the end of his life, Jones used his glass-plate negatives as cloches in the garden to protect his young plants in the early part of the growing season. Not a single Charles Jones negative is known to have survived. It is fortunate that Sean Sexton's eye helped to recognize and save the photographs, for Jones' work constitutes a quietly significant episode in the story of the millennia-old affiliation between art and natural history.

4　Albrecht Dürer
German, 1471–1528
The Great Piece of Turf, 1503
watercolor and body color
$16^{1}/_{8}$ x $12^{1}/_{2}$ in. (410 x 315 mm)

"For verily, art is embedded in Nature;
he who can extract it, has it."

Albrecht Dürer [3]

Some of the first images created by man were scenes of nature on cave walls. In the centuries to follow, art employed nature continuously. The results were variously objects of veneration, awe and scientific enlightenment. Eventually, images came to fulfill a need for simple aesthetic contemplation.

5 Giovanna Garzoni
Italian, 1600–70
A Dish of Broad Beans
gouache on parchment

The specific subject matter of the still life, however, has endured a difficult existence as an art form. The subject can be divided into two areas: the work of private investigation and reflection, and the public object of display and commerce.

Examples of the former are the brilliant natural history drawings and watercolors of Leonardo da Vinci and Albrecht Dürer (4). Inquisitive, naturalistic and totally unpretentious, these are some of the most incisive renderings of the natural world ever recorded by man.

Representative of the latter is the prominent role that the still life played in the art of seventeenth-century Italy and Holland. Symbolic of the entrepreneurial

16

6 Rembrandt
Harmensz van Rijn
Dutch, 1606–69
The Shell (Conus Marmoreus), 1650
etching, drypoint
and burin, ii/iii
3³/₄ x 5 in.
(97 x 132 mm)

opulence of those societies and often used for moralizing themes, the still life was raised to a level of importance that it never again realized. Examples of such works are an exquisite series of still-life watercolors by Giovanna Garzoni (5) and Rembrandt's only etched still life (6).

The still life as a visual record of scientific investigation gained prominence during the seventeenth, eighteenth and nineteenth centuries. This was an art that was frequently balanced between the two extremes of dispassionate reportage and aesthetic refinement. Redouté's volumes documenting various species of flowers and plants (7) and John James Audubon's *The Birds of North America* are perhaps the most familiar and magnificent examples.

7 Pierre Joseph Redouté
French, 1759–1840
Broom, 1786
grey wash and
watercolor
9⁷/₈ x 14³/₄ in.
(250 x 375 mm)

17

8 Anna Atkins
British, 1799–1871
*Aspidium
achrosticoides
(America)*, c. 1850
cyanotype
10¹/₈ x 8 in.
(258 x 202 mm)

At the beginning of the nineteenth century, advances in the fields of chemistry and optics, as well as the artistic interest of visionaries who excelled in these multidimensional areas, led to the development of photography. From the very beginning, in the earliest experiments of pioneer photographers, the depiction of nature in still lifes was divided into two areas. In the first, nature was treated as a form of dispassionate scientific evidence, as seen in the photogenic drawings by William Henry Fox Talbot and Anna Atkins (8). In the second, nature was arranged in imitation of classical still-life painting. Those who excelled in this form of controlled composition were Charles Aubry, Henri Le Secq, Adolphe Braun, Roger Fenton, James Valentine (9) and Carleton Watkins.

It is not known where or when Charles Jones created his extensive and highly focused body of work. The photographs are undated and the few photographs that are landscapes rather than still lifes do not contain architecture or landmarks that definitively locate a specific site. Nevertheless, on the basis of a still-life photograph

9　James Valentine
Scottish, 1815–80
A Heron, c. 1870
albumen print
from collodion
glass negative
9³/₈ x 7³/₈ in.
(238 x 186 mm)

10 Charles Jones
British, 1866–1959
*Garden Scene with
photographer's cloth
backdrop, c.* 1900
gold-toned gelatin
silver print
6 x 4¹/₄ in. (152 x 108 mm)

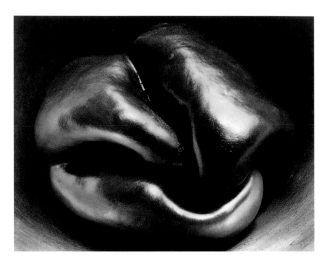

11 Edward Weston
    American, 1886–1958
    Pepper, 1930
    gelatin silver print
    7¹/₂ x 9³/₈ in.
    (191 x 238 mm)

in a family album with the date of 1904 written below it and the photographic materials used by him, a dating of 1895–1910 for the photographs is probable. Further, it is likely that these photographs were made when Jones was employed as a gardener at Ote Hall. Judging by the tone of the 1905 article in *The Gardeners' Chronicle,* Jones held a prestigious position as gardener at Ote Hall and his talents were duly noted. The fact that the article does not also mention Jones as a photographer or acknowledge the existence of a body of photographs of vegetables, fruits, or flowers could be an oversight. More likely, however, Jones considered his photographic work in still life a private creative activity and thus did not reveal it to the writer.

Charles Jones did not photograph his vegetables, fruits and flowers within nature. On the contrary, he isolated the works against neutral dark or light backgrounds (10). In their way, these set-ups are formal studio "portraits." They have all the careful lighting, pose and viewpoint of a Félix Nadar or Etienne Carjat portrait of Sarah Bernhardt or Charles Baudelaire. Jones' unique vision, however, lay in not

12 Josef Sudek
    Czechoslovakian
    1896–1976
    Still life of apple,
    1950s
    gelatin silver print
    4¹/₈ x 3³/₄ in.
    (103 x 95 mm)

succumbing to Edwardian taste for contrived compositions. His only contrivance, if one wishes to label his artistic approach as such, was an insistence on the striking isolation of his subjects. The close-up view, long exposure (to achieve depth of field and a full range of values in his subjects and their shadows) and spare arrangements anticipate later modernist photography such as the work of Edwin Hale Lincoln, August Kotzsch, Karl Blossfeldt, Edward Weston (11), Paul Outerbridge, Albert Renger-Patzsch and Josef Sudek (12). Nevertheless, just as the work of Charles Jones can be said to prefigure certain advanced still-life photography of the twentieth century, so can it be declared heir to a great British tradition in which photography is linked with fierce individuality, bordering on eccentricity. Other artists of this tradition include such photographers as William Henry Fox Talbot, Anna Atkins, Julia Margaret Cameron, Frederick Evans, Peter Henry Emerson and John Deakin. Ultimately it is impressive that, in the august company to which I have referred, the quality and consistency of his vision makes Jones one of the most original, albeit unusual, practitioners of the medium in the history of British photography.

Charles Jones left no notes, diaries or writings to explain his reasons for the creation of such a prodigious and concentrated body of photographs. The artist Peter Milton, when asked to write a statement defining his art, replied: "I would be a sad father indeed if these children weren't able to speak for themselves."[4] For Charles Jones, these photographs are almost certainly the only statement we shall ever have. Reserved, refined, humble yet eloquent, his art reveals the beauty of archetype and variance in the commonplace of nature.

Notes

1 Quoted in *Mark Adams*, Chronicle Books, San Francisco, 1985, p. 15

2 *The Gardeners' Chronicle,* September 20, 1905, pp. 249–50

3 Quoted from Baard, *Frans Hals,* 1981 in *A Dictionary of Quotations*, compiled by Ian Crofton, Schirmer Books, 1988, p. 127

4 Quoted in G. Baro, *30 Years of American Printmaking*, The Brooklyn Museum, 1976, p. 141

Charles Jones' photographs are gold-toned gelatin silver prints from glass-plate negatives. These photographs are vintage prints, *c.* 1895–1910; all those reproduced in this book are in the collection of Sean Sexton, London. No Charles Jones negatives are known to have survived.

The titles of the photographs in this volume use Jones' own graphite notations on the verso of the images. They reflect the plant nomenclature of England *c.* 1900 and might be at variance with present-day terminology.

Jones printed his photographs in three sizes. The photographs in this volume are to the following approximate dimensions:

1st Size: 6 x 4^1/$_4$ in. (152 x 108 mm) Pages: 26, 28, 30–8, 41, 43, 46–7, 52–73, 75–6, 78–83, 87–91, 94–105, 108–25

2nd Size: 8^1/$_2$ x 6^1/$_2$ in. (216 x 165 mm) Pages: 29, 42, 44, 48–9, 74, 77, 86, 92–3

3rd Size: 10 x 8 in. (254 x 203 mm) Pages: 27, 39–40, 45, 50–1, 126–7

THE PLATES

1
VEGETABLES

"By viewing Nature, Nature's handmaid, art,
Makes mighty things from small beginnings grow."

JOHN DRYDEN, *Annus Mirabilis*, 1666

Cabbage Imperial (detail of page 77)

26

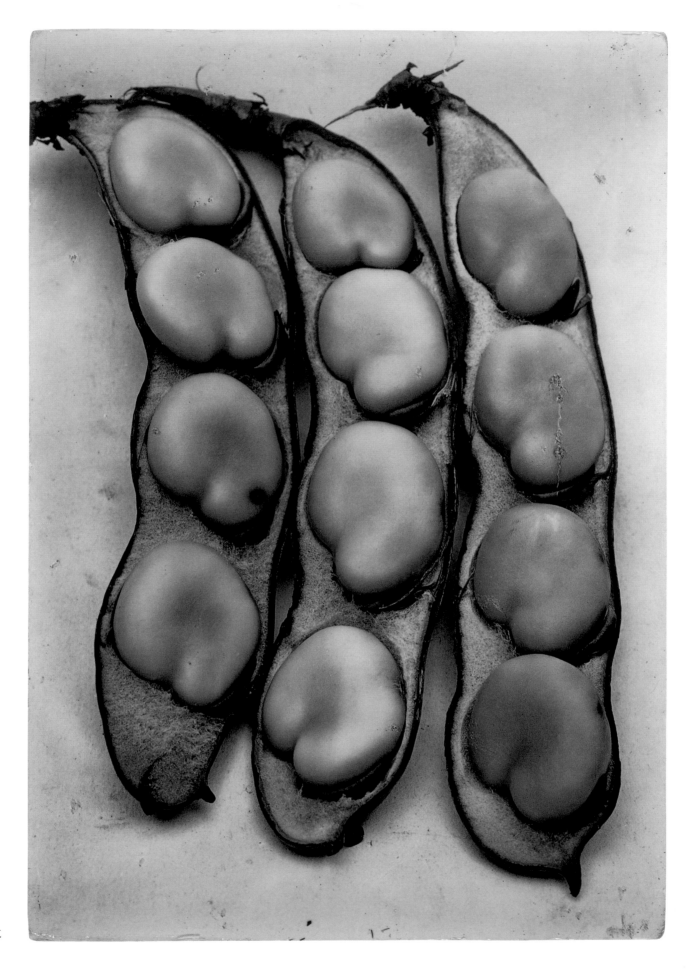

Bean Runner

Bean Runner

Bean Longpod

Bean Runner

Swede Green Top

Turnip White Milan

Pea Gladstone

Sugar Pea

34

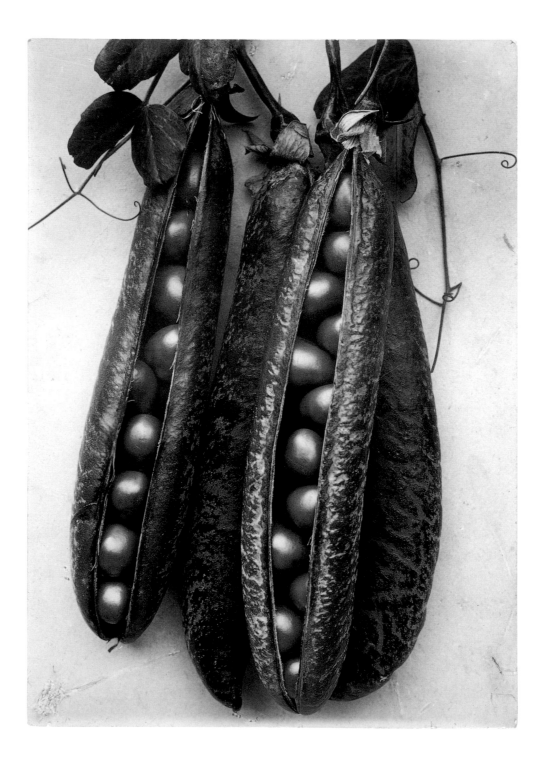

Pea Rival

Pea Early Giant

36

Onion Rousham Park Hero

Onion Brown Globe

38

Leek Prizetaker

Celery Standard Bearer

Celery Standard Bearer

Celery Wright's White

42

Vegetable Marrow Long White

43

Vegetable Marrow Long White

44

Beet Globe

Turnip Green Globe

46

Radish Red Turnip

Radish White Olive

Brussels Sprouts

49

Tomato Perfection

Potato Midlothian Early

Onion White Tripoli

52

Cucumber Ridge

53

Bean (Dwarf) Ne Plus Ultra

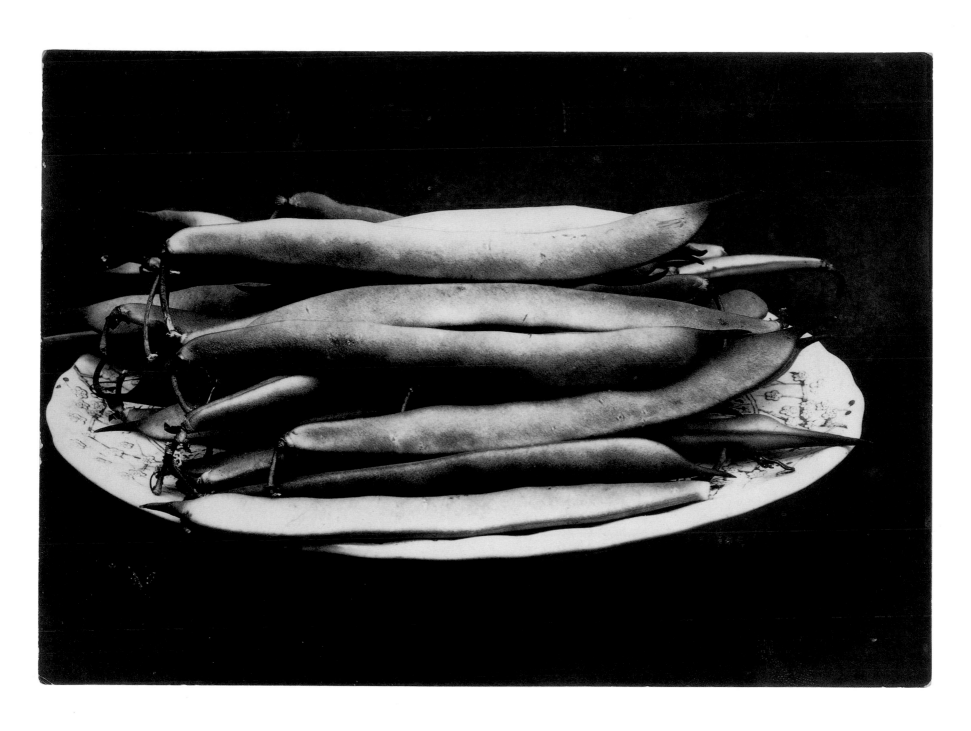

Dwarf Bean Waxpod

Vegetable Marrow Long White

Ornamental Gourds

Turnip Early Six Weeks

Beet Globe

Cabbage Lettuce

Cabbage Drumhead

62

Mangold Yellow Globe

Mangold Red Tankard

Mangold Yellow Globe

Mangold Long Red

Mangold Red Tankard

Mangold Red Tankard

Mangold Long Red

Swede Green Top

Broccoli Late Queen

Marrow Green Striped

Ornamental Gourd

Ornamental Gourd

Turnip White

Radish White Icicle

Cabbage Winnigstadt

Cabbage Imperial

78

Broccoli Snow's Winter White

Cauliflower Veitch's Autumn Giant

Larry's Perfection

82

Turnip Early Six Weeks

A Cob of Maize

2

FLOWERS

"Nature does not lie on the surface,
but hides in the depth."

Paul Cézanne

Tulip gesneriana lutea (detail of page 90)

86

Iris louisiana

Tigridia pavonia

Iceland Poppies Mixed

Hollyhocks Double

Tulip gesneriana lutea

Tulip Dom Pedro

92

Chrysanthemum F.S. Vallis

93

Hyacinth Prince Henry

Begonia Single White

Sunflower Single

Collerette Dahlia Pilot

Stokesia cyanea

Cobaea scandens

Canna

Seedpods on the head of a Standard Rose

Tritoma uvaria

Hoya carnosa (The Wax Flower)

Muscari comosum (Plumosum)

Captain Hayward

Mrs John Laing

3

FRUITS

"Beauty in art is truth bathed in an impression received
from nature. . . . While I strive for a conscientious imitation,
I yet never for an instant lose the emotion that has taken hold of me.
Reality is one part of art; feeling completes it."

CAMILLE COROT, c. 1856

Pear Beurré Rance (detail of page 111)

Plum Grand Duke

Plum Monarch

Apple Lemon Pippin

Pear Beurré Rance

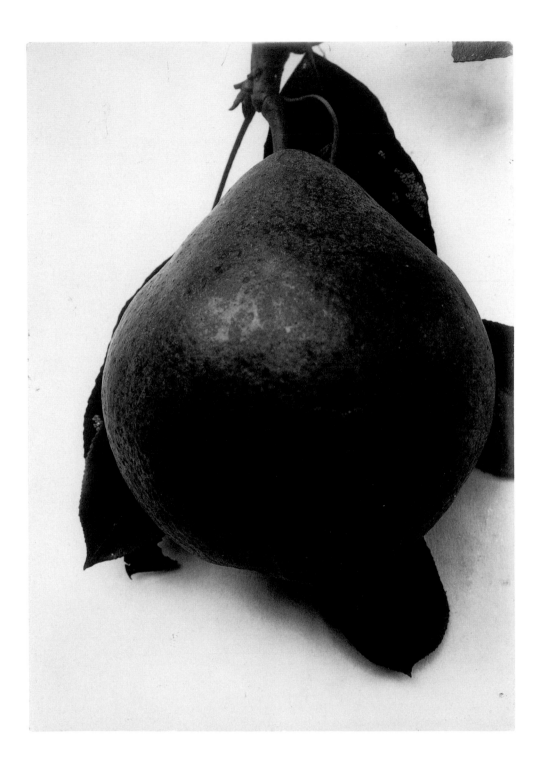

Pear Beurré Diel

Plum Monarch

114

Strawberry Leader

Quillin's Golden Gage

Apple Ecklinville Seedling

Apple Gateshead Codlin

118

Cherry Red Bigarreau

Red Currants

Crab John Downie

Gooseberry Criterion

Cherry White Heart

Arbutus unedo

Pear Beurré Diel

Pear Brockworth Park

Melon Sutton's Superlative

Melon Sutton's Superlative

Illustration Acknowledgments

1   Anonymous (British)
    Charles Jones, c. 1904
    albumen print
    6 x 4¹/₄ in. (152 x 108 mm)
    Collection of Shirley Sadler

2   Charles Jones (British, 1866–1959)
    Dwarf Beans Waxpod, c. 1900
    gold-toned gelatin silver print
    6 x 4¹/₄ in. (152 x 108 mm)
    Collection of Sean Sexton

3   Charles Jones (British, 1866–1959)
    verso of *Dwarf Beans Waxpod, c.* 1900
    gold-toned gelatin silver print
    6 x 4¹/₄ in. (152 x 108 mm)
    Collection of Sean Sexton

4   Albrecht Dürer (German, 1471–1528)
    The Great Piece of Turf, 1503
    watercolor and body color
    16¹/₈ x 12¹/₂ in. (410 x 315 mm)
    Vienna, Albertina

5   Giovanna Garzoni (Italian, 1600–70)
    A Dish of Broad Beans
    gouache on parchment
    Palazzo Pitti, Florence

6   Rembrandt Harmensz van Rijn
    (Dutch, 1606–69)
    The Shell (Conus Marmoreus), 1650
    etching, drypoint and burin, ii/iii
    3³/₄ x 5 in. (97 x 132 mm)
    Fine Arts Museums of San Francisco,
    Achenbach Foundation for Graphic Arts;
    purchase, anonymous gift, and gift of
    Dr. T. Edward and Tullah Hanley by exchange

7   Pierre Joseph Redouté (French, 1759–1840)
    Broom, 1786
    grey wash and watercolor
    9⁷/₈ x 14³/₄ in. (250 x 375 mm)

    Fine Arts Museums of San Francisco,
    Achenbach Foundation for Graphic Arts;
    purchase, and gift of Phoebe Cowles and
    Mark, Michael, and Lawrence Gibson

8   Anna Atkins (British, 1799–1871)
    Aspidium achrosticoides (America), c. 1850
    cyanotype
    10¹/₈ x 8 in. (258 x 202 mm)
    Fine Arts Museums of San Francisco,
    Achenbach Foundation for Graphic Arts;
    Mrs. Milton S. Latham Fund

9   James Valentine (Scottish, 1815–80)
    A Heron, c. 1870
    albumen print from collodion glass negative
    9³/₈ x 7³/₈ in. (238 x 186 mm)
    Fine Arts Museums of San Francisco,
    Achenbach Foundation for Graphic Arts;
    Mrs. Milton S. Latham Fund

10 Charles Jones (British, 1866–1959)
    Garden Scene with photographer's cloth backdrop
    c. 1900
    gold-toned gelatin silver print
    6 x 4¹/₄ in. (152 x 108 mm)
    Collection of Sean Sexton

11 Edward Weston (American, 1886–1958)
    Pepper, 1930
    gelatin silver print
    7¹/₂ x 9³/₈ in. (191 x 238 mm)
    San Francisco Museum of Modern Art,
    Albert M. Bender Collection, Albert
    M. Bender Bequest Fund Purchase 62.1166
    © 1981 Center for Creative Photography,
    Arizona Board of Regents

12 Josef Sudek (Czechoslovakian, 1896–1976)
    Still life of apple, 1950s
    gelatin silver print,
    4¹/₈ x 3³/₄ in. (103 x 95 mm)
    Courtesy Christies, London